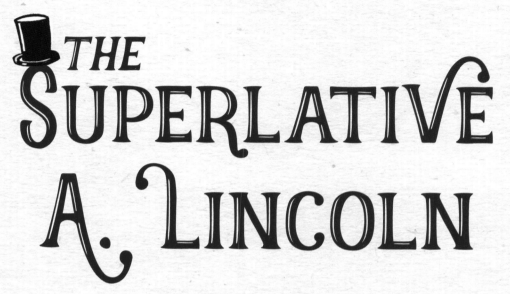

THE SUPERLATIVE A. LINCOLN

POEMS ABOUT OUR 16TH PRESIDENT

EILEEN R. MEYER

ILLUSTRATED BY
DAVE SZALAY

Charlesbridge

CONTENTS

superlative (*suh-PUR-luh-tiv* or *soo-PUR-luh-tiv*)

adjective
1. of the best or highest quality; supreme.
2. having to do with adjectives or adverbs that show the highest or lowest degree of comparison, such as *tallest, worst,* and *most likely.*

noun
1. a superlative person or thing.
2. the greatest degree of something.
3. an adjective or adverb in the superlative degree, such as *the tallest* or *the most likely.*

SIMPLY SUPERLATIVE

Come read about a legend—
the greatest of the greats;
from a poor boy in the backwoods
to a president, first-rate.

Just how was he outstanding?
How did he top the rest?
What was it that inspired this man
to do his very best?

Come get to know Abe Lincoln.
You'll find new stories here.
You'll see that he's *SUPERLATIVE*
in many ways—it's clear!

Abraham Lincoln was born in a one-room log cabin on February 12, 1809. Rising from the *humblest* beginnings, he became one of the *most celebrated* leaders in our nation's history. As one of our *greatest* presidents, he strove to reach lofty goals. What challenges did he face? What made him so remarkable? These stories just might surprise you.

MOST STUDIOUS
Yearning to Learn

Abe's schools weren't open
through the year—
a few weeks there or one month here.

So he kept learnin'
on his own.
No internet. No telephone.

He borrowed books.
He farmed and read—
and pondered stories in his head.

He read the same
books every night.
He scribbled notes by candlelight.

No private school.
No framed degree.
Self-learning was Abe's pedigree!

Amazingly, Abraham Lincoln had less than one year of formal schooling during his entire childhood. As Lincoln put it, his school attendance was "by littles"—a month one year, a few weeks another year. Many years there was no school offered at all in the part of rural Indiana where he grew up. His thirst for knowledge and his curiosity about the world drove him to learn all he could. Lincoln was truly a self-educated man.

MOST DISTRACTED FARMER
What He'd Rather Do

He's one distracted farmer.
He'd readily agree:
he'd like to chuck his farm chores.
He'd rather sit and read.

He stops with each new furrow.
The plow horse takes a rest.
A book pops from Abe's pocket:
a story to digest.

He clears a neighbor's timber.
Then splits rails one by one,
while memorizing passages
beneath the blazing sun.

He feeds a restless hunger.
Words call to him—*Come look!*
He hunts for pearls of wisdom
inside a borrowed book.

He's one distracted farmer.
He'd readily agree:
he'd like to chuck his farm chores.
He'd rather sit and read.

Thomas Lincoln hired out his son Abraham to neighbors as a farmhand. Young Abe was paid to do grueling work: plowing, clearing land, splitting logs for rail fences, and more. He quickly realized that a life of hard labor was not for him— he wanted to read and study instead. His stepmother, Sarah, supported him. She eventually convinced Thomas to allow Abe more time to study. "The things I want to know is in books," Abe said. "My best friend's the man who'll git me one."

BEST LUMBERJACK
Lincoln and His Ax

As he toiled to fell a great tree,
his talent was something to see.
With each swing of his blade,
he was far underpaid,
for young Abe did the labor of three!

Abraham Lincoln learned to use an ax when he was eight years old. He helped his father clear land and build a log cabin for their family. As Lincoln grew, his ax was his constant companion. He developed a powerful swing and became extraordinarily fit. A friend noted, "If you heard him fellin' trees in a clearin', you would say there were three men at work the way the trees fell."

BIGGEST DREAMER
How Lincoln Earned Two Silver Half-Dollars

*H*e was no ordinary teen—
a brainy boy, built tall and lean.
He chopped.
And chopped.
And chopped some more.
He helped his pa. Their kin were poor.
He used his hands. Why not his head?
Could he do something else instead?

One afternoon, two men approached.
They had to catch that riverboat!
Could Abe provide a ferry ride?
He rowed them to the steamboat's side.
A few strong strokes—Abe's work was through.
The businessmen called out, "Thank you."
They tossed two coins—a silver prize.
Young Abe could not believe his eyes.
For just one ride—this hefty fee?
Now Abe saw opportunity.

Abe's world looked brighter from that day.
Soon he would leave and make his way.
For now
he chopped
but knew he'd find
pursuits where he could use his mind.
A skillful lad, astute and keen—
he was no ordinary teen.

incoln typically earned twenty-five cents a day splitting wood—tiring, backbreaking work. One day two businessmen paid him a whole dollar for simply giving them a ride. Earning such a large amount so easily had a huge impact on the seventeen-year-old Lincoln's dreams. "You may think it was a very little thing," he later remembered, "but it was a most important incident in my life. I could scarcely credit that I, a poor boy, had earned a dollar in less than a day. . . . The world seemed wider and fairer before me." Soon he would set out on his own and seek new opportunities.

BEST WRESTLER
Tips from the Champ

Talk bold and loud.
Attract a crowd.
Claim you're the best.
Take on the rest.
Rip off your shirt.
Stomp in the dirt.
Spread arms out wide.
Move quick and slide.
Act rough and tough.
Then call their bluff.
Look fierce and frown.
Then throw 'em down.
Don't crack a grin
(until you win).
Extend a hand
to help 'em stand.
So all can see
sweet VICTORY!

Believe it or not, our sixteenth president is in the National Wrestling Hall of Fame. A former director of the Hall of Fame noted, "Lincoln undoubtedly was the roughest and toughest of the wrestling Presidents." As a young man, Lincoln stood six feet four inches tall, weighed 185 pounds, and was muscular and long-armed. He took on all challengers and rarely lost a match. Frontier wrestling matches were rough-and-tumble bouts that ended when one wrestler threw another off his feet. They say Lincoln was a good sport, always helping his opponent up after winning the match.

MOST RESPECTED
Lincoln's Boot Camp

They march
and drill—
left, right, left, right.

They stand
their post.
Keep watch all night.

They make
their beds
and shine their boots.

To Captain
Lincoln
they salute.

They are a splendid
army corps—

    but never spent a day at war!

During the Black Hawk War of 1832, Lincoln served as a soldier for three months. His peers elected him a militia captain, which he later said was one of the most satisfying honors of his life. Poking fun at himself, Lincoln recalled that he survived "a good many bloody struggles with the musquetoes." His troops never saw action, but the experience was invaluable.

MOST LIKELY TO TINKER
Notes Regarding A. Lincoln's Invention

How Created:
clever mind

When Accomplished:
daily grind

Education:
self-made man

How He Started:
hatched a plan

Work Submitted:
model boat

His Invention:
helps it float

If Successful:
pays the rent

Other Prospects:
president

Abraham Lincoln is the only US president to hold a patent for an invention. As a young man, he worked for a time on various rivers. One day his flatboat got stuck and started taking on water. Thinking quickly, Lincoln bored a hole in the front of the boat, which hung out over a low dam. Shifting the cargo forward tilted the boat so the water could drain out. Lincoln plugged the hole and saved the day—and the cargo.

Years later, after he became a lawyer, Lincoln tinkered some more with this idea. His design to help boats float over shallow river spots was awarded Patent No. 6469.

Best Advice
Why Not Whiskers?

Dear Mr. Lincoln,

A candidate should look his best,
so kindly hear my bold request.
You're very tall and awful thin.
You need some whiskers on your chin.
Just keep in mind the time you'll save
when you no longer need to shave.
I think most ladies will take note
and urge the men to cast their votes.
Please grow a beard. I hope you do.
We need a leader just like you.

Sincerely,

Grace Bedell

Did you know that Abraham Lincoln was the first president to wear a beard? In October 1860 eleven-year-old Grace Bedell wrote to presidential candidate Lincoln. She suggested that he grow a beard because "all the ladies like whiskers and they would tease their husbands to vote for you and then you would be president." (Women were not allowed to vote during this time.) Lincoln won the election and soon after began to grow his distinctive beard. During his travels, he met with young Grace to thank her for the letter.

BEST YARN-SPINNER
The President Tells a Story

*H*e'd tell you a joke.
He'd share an old tale.
He'd spin a new story
with folksy detail.

He'd chuckle and laugh
at his wisecracking, then
give light to the truth
as he made a new friend.

Like stars in the sky,
like bright flecks of gold,
his words shone long after
his stories were told.

*A*braham Lincoln was a master at spinning stories and yarns. The poet Walt Whitman said Lincoln's storytelling was "a weapon which he employ'd with great skill." He frequently used folksy stories to calm an opponent, illustrate a point, or drive home an important truth. He also liked joking around—especially at his own expense. The president was a sight to behold while telling his stories: his face beamed, he was animated, and when he delivered the punch line, his high-pitched laughter sounded throughout the room.

Most Permissive Parent
The Lincoln Boys at Play

*T*hey're . . .
fast-as-lightning streakers,
White House hide-and-seekers,
around-the-corner peekers.
>*They're undercover spies!*

They're . . .
across-the-wood-floor gliders,
stairway-railing sliders,
hallway horsey-riders.
>*They're galloping nearby!*

They're . . .
Lincoln's main attraction,
a welcome work distraction,
a father's greatest passion, and
>*the apples of his eye!*

*A*braham Lincoln and his wife, Mary, doted on their sons. Abraham Lincoln was relaxed in his approach to parenting. He said, "It is my pleasure that my children are free, happy and unrestrained by parental tyranny." Youngest sons Willie and Tad had spirited adventures after moving into the White House. They ran wild in the halls and adopted a menagerie of animals, including cats, rabbits, goats, ponies, at least one dog, and a turkey.

WORST ROOM NAME
The Lincoln Bedroom

There was no bed.
The record's clear.
He *never* slept a wink in here.

No patchwork quilt.
No cotton sheets.
No fuzzy slippers for Abe's feet.

No flannel jams.
No dressing gowns.
No counting sheep. No snoring sounds.

Within these walls
he wrote and read.
Whyever would he need a bed?

This White House room is called the Lincoln Bedroom, even though Abraham Lincoln *didn't* sleep in it. Instead, he used the space as his office and held many important meetings there. In 1945 the room was renovated and furnished in part with bedroom furniture bought by Mary Lincoln. No one knows if the furniture was ever used by the president, but people began calling the room the Lincoln Bedroom anyway. Many visitors to the room claim to have experienced ghost sightings of the former president.

BEST USE OF AN ACCESSORY

Lincoln's Stovepipe Hat Speaks Out

We don't need a leather briefcase.
We don't want an attaché.
You can keep that canvas knapsack.
I'm a traveling valet.

Abe writes notes upon my flat top.
He tucks letters in my band.
I'm his silken compact office,
and I'm always close at hand.

Abraham Lincoln and his stovepipe hat were a team. He used his headwear to carry letters, notes, and documents when he was out of the office, tucking the items inside the lining. The hat's flat top proved useful as a writing surface, allowing Lincoln to jot down notes on the go. The hat also highlighted his great height advantage over others and protected him from harsh weather.

STRONGEST CONVICTION
Signing the Emancipation Proclamation

*S*ummer 1862

The nation was divided
as the Civil War raged on.
The problem Lincoln grappled with:
to right the greatest wrong.

He gathered his advisors, said,
No man is property.
He would proclaim in rebel states,
Those held as slaves are FREE.

His proclamation fueled debate.
Some folks did not agree.
Is freedom meant for everyone
in our democracy?

New Year's Day 1863

Crowds streamed in past the White House gates
to greet the president.
He stood for hours to shake each hand,
express acknowledgment.

When guests were gone, he grasped his pen
and sat up straight and tall.
He s–l–o–w–l–y, *firmly* signed his name.
Now liberty for *ALL*.

Abraham Lincoln considered the Emancipation Proclamation to be one of the most important achievements of his administration. This executive order freed people held as slaves in states that had seceded from the United States.

In July 1862 Lincoln shared the draft of the proclamation with his cabinet. In the following months, people all over the country debated whether Lincoln would actually issue it. Exhausted after shaking hands for hours at a New Year's Day reception, Lincoln noticed his hand quivering as he prepared to sign the proclamation. "Now, this signature is one that will be closely examined," he said, "and if they find my hand trembled, they will say 'he had some compunctions.'" He firmly and carefully signed his full name. "I never, in my life, felt more certain that I was doing right, than I do in signing this paper."

MOST SURPRISING FRIENDSHIP
Frederick Douglass and Abraham Lincoln

Two men first meet—

one black,

one white.

Two different views.

Could both be right?

One presses for
equality.

One seeks to heal
disunity.

A friendship buds
when each man finds
the other has
an open mind.

Frederick Douglass was a famous speaker, newspaper editor, author, abolitionist, and former slave. At times he was also a critic of President Lincoln. On August 10, 1863, Douglass made a surprise visit to the White House. A crowd was already waiting to see Lincoln, but the president welcomed Douglass and invited him to talk privately. Douglass urged the president to provide equal treatment for black troops serving in the Union Army. Lincoln explained that he was moving toward equal rights as fast as he thought the country could handle. Although they disagreed, Lincoln and Douglass admired and respected each other. Later, Lincoln told Douglass, "There is no man in the country whose opinion I value more than yours."

GREATEST SPEECH
Lincoln's Gettysburg Address

Superb.
Profound.
A work of art.
The perfect speech—
it stands apart.
It soars.
It rings.
We hold it dear.
But . . .
     it wasn't what folks came to hear!

Did you know that Abraham Lincoln was *not* the featured speaker at the dedication of the Gettysburg National Cemetery? Edward Everett, a famous Massachusetts orator, was the main speaker and talked for over two hours. President Lincoln spoke for only two minutes and delivered what author Carl Sandburg called the "great American poem." His short speech has become an American classic and is celebrated for its beauty and simplicity.

score and seven years ago our fathers brought
upon this continent, a new nation, conceived
liberty, and dedicated to the proposition that
men are created equal".

we are engaged in a great civil war, testing
ther that nation any nation so conceived,
so ded

LEAST FAVORITE NICKNAME
Greeting Guidelines

Call him Mr. President,
the leader of our states.
Call him a great orator,
well known for his debates.
Call him neighbor, father, son—
all labels he could claim.
Know that when folks called him Abe,
he didn't like *that* name.

Nicknamed Abe during childhood, Abraham Lincoln preferred other forms of address as an adult. His friends called him Lincoln or Mr. Lincoln. Even his wife called him Mr. Lincoln. When he became president, people called him Mr. President, of course. He signed his name "Abraham Lincoln" or "A. Lincoln." Even though Lincoln didn't like his childhood nickname, we still call him Abe today. Why? Maybe it's because that nickname fits our idea of Lincoln as a folksy, regular guy—one of us.

WHO'S TALLEST?
Presidential Stature

Obama, Trump—both stand up tall,
but neither's tallest of them all.
LBJ—he stretched up high!
These other leaders scraped the sky:
Clinton, Arthur, Jefferson,
Bush (the first), and Washington,
Reagan, Jackson, FDR—
yet none of them could set the bar.
At six-foot-four, you may conclude,
Lincoln reached TOP altitude.
Of Oval Office employees
he towered HIGH in history!

Abraham Lincoln was our tallest president. During the Civil War era, the average man was only five feet seven inches tall. At six feet four inches, Lincoln measured a whopping nine inches taller than that mark. He was literally a giant among the men of his day.

Other presidents who stood tall include, in order of height: Lyndon B. Johnson (LBJ), Donald J. Trump, Thomas Jefferson, George Washington, Chester A. Arthur, Franklin D. Roosevelt (FDR), George H. W. Bush, William J. Clinton, Andrew Jackson, Ronald Reagan, and Barack Obama.

In case you were wondering, the shortest president, James Madison, stood only five feet four inches.

6 feet, 4 inches

5 feet, 4 inches

Barack Obama

Abraham Lincoln

George Washington

James Madison

MOST ADMIRED PRESIDENT
Why Do We Cherish Abraham Lincoln?

Because he rose from modest means—
    though poor, he showed you can
    aim high and serve as president:
    our greatest self-made man.

Because he bravely mended our
    once frayed democracy
    and took a stand proclaiming
    that all people should be free.

Because he showed great wisdom
    in a time of war and strife—
    he gave his heart, he gave us hope,
    and then he gave his life.

Because he is *SUPERLATIVE*,
    we praise his legacy.
    Our Lincoln is a symbol of
    the best that we can be.

Each year millions of people visit the Lincoln Memorial in Washington, DC. It is one of the most beloved US national monuments. Lincoln's story of growing up poor in rural America, far from the seat of government, provides hope to people from all walks of life and from all corners of the country. We admire how this plainspoken man led the nation in a time of crisis. For people all over the world, Abraham Lincoln is a timeless symbol of democracy.

AUTHOR'S NOTE

Abraham Lincoln's legacy is all around us: his profile appears on the pennies that jingle in our pockets, his portrait graces the five-dollar bills tucked inside our wallets, and his name appears on roads and schools across the country.

An avid Lincoln admirer, I read widely about our sixteenth president for this project and explored places that were important to his life's journey. I meandered around New Salem, Illinois, where Lincoln served as postmaster and developed the habit of storing letters inside his hat. I strolled streets near his law office in Springfield, Illinois, where he likely swapped stories with friends. I marveled at the model of his 1849 patent invention at a museum in Washington, DC. I scaled the steps of the Lincoln Memorial and watched visitors from all over the world stare in wonder at his marble likeness. By experiencing these places, viewing important artifacts, and speaking with historians, I formed a deeper understanding of this humble and heroic man.

It was an exciting challenge to consider Lincoln's many life experiences, then craft a series of poems that would hopefully engage and delight readers. Telling a story within the spare framework of a poem using pleasing sounds, rhythms, and language is something I greatly enjoy. It was especially fun writing a poem from the stovepipe hat's point of view and adding a little sassiness to its voice. I hope these poems spark interest in Lincoln's life and inspire you to learn more. And perhaps you might even pen your own poem about Lincoln.

THE SUPERLATIVE YOU

Abraham Lincoln was superlative in many ways. During his childhood, he was the most studious member of his family. As a young man, he was the best wrestler in the county. In what ways are you superlative?

Best Sport

Best Friend

Best Dancer

Biggest Class Clown

Best Storyteller

Bravest

Biggest Dreamer

Most Artistic

Calmest

Most Caring

Most Daring

Most Athletic

Most Likely to Become Famous

Most Likely to Become a Teacher

Most Likely to Break a World Record

Most Likely to Travel the World

Most Likely to Become President

Most Outgoing

Most Likely to Invent Something

Most Studious

Most Talkative

Most Organized

Most Trustworthy

Most School Spirit

Youngest

Oldest

Friendliest

Time Line of Abraham Lincoln's Life

1809 Born February 12 in a one-room log cabin in Kentucky to Thomas and Nancy Hanks Lincoln.

1815 Briefly attends school with his sister, Sarah.

1816 Family moves near Little Pigeon Creek, Indiana.

1817 Learns to use an ax and helps his father build another log cabin.

1818 Mother dies. Life is very difficult in rural Indiana.

1819 Father remarries. Stepmother Sarah Bush Johnston Lincoln is kind and loving to Abe.

EARLY 1820s
Works on family farm. Attends school a few times. Borrows books to read and learn.

1826 Hired out to work for other farmers. Becomes a highly skilled woodsman.

1826 Earns a whole dollar for ferrying businessmen on the Ohio River and sees new opportunities.

1830 Family moves to Illinois, settling on Sangamon River near Decatur.

1831 Moves out on his own to New Salem, Illinois.
Works as a store clerk and performs other odd jobs. Known as a formidable wrestler.

1832 Enlists in the Illinois militia and is elected captain of his company during the Black Hawk War.
Runs for the Illinois legislature and loses.

1833 Appointed postmaster in New Salem, Illinois. Uses his hat to store letters while making deliveries to distant residents.

1834 Elected to the Illinois legislature, where he serves four terms.

1834–1836
Studies on his own and becomes a lawyer.

1837 Moves to Springfield, Illinois.

1842 Marries Mary Todd.

1843 First son, Robert, is born.
Withdraws name for congressional-seat nomination in favor of a friend.

1844 Starts law practice with partner William Herndon. Known as "Honest Abe" for his work ethic and honesty as a lawyer.

1846 Second son, Edward, is born. The family calls him Eddy (often spelled Eddie). Elected to the US House of Representatives; serves one term. Continues to read and study, now using the Library of Congress.

1849 Awarded Patent No. 6469 for a device he invented to help boats float over shallow river spots.

1850 Son Eddy dies after a long illness. Third son, William (called Willie), is born.

1853 Fourth son, Thomas (called Tad), is born.

1856 Helps form the Republican Party in Illinois.

1858 Campaigns for US Senate and debates Stephen Douglas throughout Illinois; loses but gains national attention.

1860 Elected sixteenth president of the United States. Grows his famous beard. South Carolina secedes from the Union on December 20.

1861 Sworn in as president on March 4.
Ten other Southern states secede and form the Confederate States of America. The Civil War begins.

1862 The Civil War rages on.
Son Willie dies.

1863 Issues Emancipation Proclamation on New Year's Day.
Meets with abolitionist Frederick Douglass at the White House.
Delivers Gettysburg Address on November 19.

1864 Elected to a second term as president.

1865 The Thirteenth Amendment abolishing slavery is passed by Congress on January 31.
Confederate forces surrender on April 9. The Civil War is over.
Shot by John Wilkes Booth while watching a play in Washington, DC, on April 14. Dies the following day.
The Thirteenth Amendment is ratified on December 6, becoming the law of the land.

1922 The Lincoln Memorial is dedicated in Washington, DC. These words are displayed above Lincoln's statue:

IN THIS TEMPLE
AS IN THE HEARTS OF THE PEOPLE
FOR WHOM HE SAVED THE UNION
THE MEMORY OF ABRAHAM LINCOLN
IS ENSHRINED FOREVER

Resources for Young Lincoln Fans

BOOKS

Fleming, Candace. *The Lincolns: A Scrapbook Look at Abraham and Mary.* New York: Schwartz & Wade, 2008.

Freedman, Russell. *Abraham Lincoln & Frederick Douglass: The Story Behind an American Friendship.* New York: Clarion, 2012.

——. *Lincoln: A Photobiography.* New York: Clarion, 1987.

Jackson, Ellen. *Abe Lincoln Loved Animals.* New York: Albert Whitman, 2008.

Keating, Frank. *Abraham.* New York: Simon & Schuster, 2017.

Krull, Kathleen, and Paul Brewer. *Lincoln Tells a Joke: How Laughter Saved the President (and the Country).* New York: Houghton Mifflin Harcourt, 2010.

Rappaport, Doreen. *Abe's Honest Words: The Life of Abraham Lincoln.* New York: Hyperion, 2008.

Schroeder, Alan. *Abe Lincoln: His Wit and Wisdom from A–Z.* New York: Holiday House, 2015.

Wells, Rosemary. *Lincoln and His Boys.* Somerville, MA: Candlewick, 2009.

WEBSITES

Abraham Lincoln Birthplace National Historical Park: http://www.nps.gov/abli
History relating to Lincoln's Kentucky birthplace.

Abraham Lincoln Presidential Library and Museum: http://www.illinois.gov/alplm/library
Documents, manuscripts, newspapers, oral biographies, and more relating to Lincoln's life.

Abraham Lincoln's Classroom: http://www.abrahamlincolnsclassroom.org
Quotes, quizzes, maps, and many other resources for students and teachers.

Lincoln Memorial: http://www.nps.gov/linc
History and information about this famous landmark in Washington, DC.

Lincoln/Net: http://lincoln.lib.niu.edu
Historical documents from the years Lincoln lived in Illinois (1830–1861).

Mr. Lincoln's White House: http://www.mrlincolnswhitehouse.org
Interesting details about Lincoln's years as president.

The URLs listed here were accurate at publication, but websites often change. If a URL doesn't work, you can use the internet to find more information.

Quotation Sources

For more information about the sources below, please see the bibliography on the next page.

Page 6: "by littles": Lincoln, *The Collected Works of Abraham Lincoln*, vol. 4, p. 62.

Page 9: "The things I . . . one": Lincoln quoted in Atkinson, p. 364.

Page 10: "If you heard . . . fell": Lincoln acquaintance quoted in Thomas, pp. 144–145.

Page 13: "You may think . . . me": Lincoln quoted in Carpenter, pp. 97–98.

Page 14: "Lincoln undoubtedly was . . . Presidents": Dellinger.

Page 16: "a good many . . . musquetoes": Lincoln, *Collected Works*, vol. 1, p. 510.